SPIRITUAL PERFECTION

Stephen Kaung

ISBN: 978-1-942521-55-6

Available from:

Christian Testimony Ministry
4424 Huguenot Road
Richmond, Virginia 23235

www.christiantestimonyministry.com

Printed in USA

CONTENTS

PREFACE

The following ministry was given by Brother Stephen Kaung at the Northeast Christian Weekend Conference, in October 2004. The theme for the conference was *Spiritual Perfection.* The conference concluded with a question and answer period, which is included as the last chapter.

The spoken messages have been transcribed into this booklet with minimal editing done for clarity, while maintaining the spoken form.

WHAT IS SPIRITUAL PERFECTION?

Matthew 5:48—Be ye therefore perfect as your heavenly Father is perfect.

Shall we pray:

Dear Lord, how we praise and thank Thee that in Thy great love towards us Thou hast gathered us together. Lord, our hearts bow before Thee. What hast Thou to say to us? Speak, Lord, Thy servants heareth. Dear Lord, we acknowledge that in ourselves there is neither understanding nor power, but we know that Thou art our wisdom and our power. So we look to Thee that Thou wilt breathe upon Thy written Word and make it living, working in our lives, that Thou may be glorified. Take away any preconceived ideas and show us Thy truth and lead us into Thy truth. We want Thee to be glorified in the midst of Thy redeemed. We ask in Thy precious name. Amen.

I believe when you read the Bible, you cannot help but see that in the Word of God there are so many places where the word *perfect* is used. And when you read that word, do you sometimes wonder what God means by this word *perfect*? So as we gather together before the Lord, we look to Him to show us what He really means when He said, "Be ye perfect as your heavenly Father is perfect."

OLD TESTAMENT PERFECTION

As you go through the Word of God, you find this word *perfect* is used not only in the New Testament but also in the Old Testament. The first mention of this word *perfect* is found in Genesis 6:9. God said, "Noah was a just man, perfect amongst his generation." What does it mean? Was Noah sinless-perfect? If you read the preceding verse you will find that Noah found favor before God. In other words, it is by the grace of God that he was considered as perfect, and it is a perfection among his generation.

Again, in Genesis 17:1, God said to Abram: "I am the Almighty God, the all-sufficient God: walk before me and be perfect." What does it mean when God said, "Walk before Me and be perfect"? We know that by faith Abram came out of Ur of Chaldea. He followed the Lord, not knowing where he was going but knowing that God was leading him. But afterwards, you find in his sojourn in Canaan he was weakened in his faith. Instead of waiting for the Lord to fulfill His promise to him, he accepted human ways; he tried to help the Lord. And it was after this that God appeared to him and said, "I am the all-sufficient God. You walk before Me and be perfect." In other words, he failed. He was imperfect in his faith, and God said, "Be perfect in your faith. Trust in Me wholly and completely."

Again, we find in the case of Job 1:1 it says, "Job was perfect and upright, and one that feared God and abstained from evil." Was Job sinless-perfect? In Job 9:1 he asked a question: "How can man be just with God?" In the following verses he said, "If I justify myself, my own mouth will condemn me. Were I perfect, God will show me I am not. If I insist on saying I am perfect, I am deceiving myself" (see verses 20-21).

So what is meant by this word *perfect*? In Deuteronomy 18:13 God said to the children of Israel: "Be perfect before Jehovah your God." All the commandments of God were supposed to be kept, and if they kept them they would be considered as perfect before God.

In the case of David, in his song in II Samuel 22:24 he said, "I was upright before him." And the word *upright* means "perfect." Was David perfect? We all know he was not sinless-perfect, but thank God he had a heart for God. He was a man after God's own heart and he would do all God's will. So in II Chronicles 16:9 it says, "The eyes of the Lord run to and fro through the whole earth, to shew himself strong in the behalf of those whose heart is perfect toward him." So evidently, David was a person who was considered as perfect in heart.

As you go through the Old Testament, you find that these people were not sinless-perfect. God is absolutely perfect, perfect in every way. But man, no matter how perfect he may be considered by God, cannot be compared with the absolute perfection of God. In Old Testament time, it was by the grace of God and the working of God in their lives to bring them to a place where they began to manifest some character like God. It was the working of God in their lives, and when God saw these things, He considered it as perfect.

A PERFECT LIFE DEMONSTRATED

In the New Testament you discover one thing. Not only is perfection the teaching of the New Testament, but God has demonstrated His perfection on earth through His beloved Son, our Lord Jesus Christ. When our Lord came into this world, He declares His Father to us. He shows us what kind of a God we have. Our God is a perfect God. He is perfect in love; He is perfect in holiness; He is perfect in righteousness; He is perfect in purity; He is perfect in wisdom; He is perfect in power. He is perfect in everything. Our God is absolutely perfect, and this is demonstrated in the life of our Lord Jesus.

There is a difference between the Old Testament and the New Testament. In the Old Testament time we find that God did work. He did give grace and favor to man, and out of His working and favor, some people were considered as perfect. But in the New Testament we come to a very different scene. Why? First of all, God came into this world to demonstrate perfection to us. That perfection is absolute, without measure, and we find this in the life of our Lord Jesus. He brought heaven upon this earth. He showed us what kind of God we have.

Some people try to imitate Christ. Now if you do not try to imitate Him, you may think that you are quite like Him. But the more you really, sincerely, honestly try to imitate Christ, to be like Him, I believe your conscience will tell you that you are far, far away from Him.

If our Lord Jesus lived on this earth for thirty-three and some years, showing us what perfection is, and then He had returned to heaven, what would happen to us? His perfect life would be our condemnation. You remember He said, "When the Holy Spirit comes, He shall convict you of sin, of righteousness, and of judgment; of righteousness because I go to the Father." In other words, no one can go to the Father except those who are as perfect as the Father. Our Lord Jesus is perfect; He is sinless-perfect. He does not know what sin is because He had never sinned. He is always obedient to the Father; He always pleased the Father. And if He had come without going to the cross and had gone back to heaven He would forever be our condemnation, because aside from Him no one can go to the Father. If anyone would try, he would be smitten to death.

LIFE RELEASED THROUGH THE CROSS

But thank God, our Lord Jesus not only came to demonstrate the perfection of God and live a perfect life, showing us what a perfect life is, but He also went to the cross. There on the cross He bore our sins; He shed His blood for the remission of our sins, that we may be justified before God. Not only that, He poured out His life for us and to us. So anyone who believes in the Lord Jesus has his sins all forgiven. "Though your sins be as scarlet they shall be as white as snow." Thank God for that!

But salvation is more than that. There is something very positive in salvation because by His death He released His life and gave His life to everyone who believes in Him. So thank God, we who believe in the Lord Jesus have eternal life.

Eternal life is not something just for the future. Eternal life begins today.

What is eternal life? Eternal life is nothing but the life of our Lord Jesus. So the most precious thing is that we have His life. He has given His very life to us. What kind of life is that? It is a perfect life and it has been demonstrated on earth as a Person. So first of all we need to remember that we who believe in the Lord Jesus have a perfect life in us, as perfect as God is perfect. You cannot be more perfect than that.

And that life is a complete life. That life has lived on this earth before. It has demonstrated His quality and His very mature life and experiential life. A life of perfection is now in you and me. Can you believe it? Sometimes you feel it is just too good, but it is true. The life that you receive is not an imperfect life because it is the very life of our Lord Jesus. That is the reason why our Lord Jesus teaches us that we need to be perfect, as the heavenly Father is perfect. But does it mean that because of this, even here on earth we can be sinless-perfect? Our Lord Jesus was sinless-perfect while He was on earth. We have His life in us and we are called to be perfect. Now why is it that we are not sinless-perfect?

SINLESS PERFECTION

When I was saved, I was saved among the holiness people who believed in so-called "second blessing." The first blessing is that you repent, you believe in the Lord Jesus, and you are saved. But you need a second blessing, which is the eradication, the uprooting of sin. You need another blessing, an experience, and through that blessing the sin nature, the root of sin in you is uprooted. So after that you will sin no more; you will be sinless-perfect. Now I was saved among these people. I think it would be very good if it were true. I think we all are bothered by sin even after we are saved. Thank God, we know that our past sins were all forgiven, but unfortunately, we find that even though we are saved we are still not only prone to sin but we do sin. It would be untrue to say that we are sinless-perfect. So our problem is how can we be sinless-perfect?

In our natural mind sin is the biggest problem, even though in the heart of God that is not the biggest problem. But to us it is the biggest problem. So when we think of perfection, immediately we think of sinless perfection. Anything less than that is not perfection. But I have to tell you, during that conference where I was saved, the founder of that mission lost her temper in public. But there was an explanation. The explanation was that it was not sin; it was weakness. Now I cannot see the difference between sin and weakness although some people do. The Bible never teaches sinless perfection. There is only one person on earth who is sinless-perfect, and that is our Lord Jesus.

Why are we not sinless-perfect? We have His very life in us. It is such a perfect life demonstrated, lived in this world before. And God expects us to be perfect. So why is it we are not sinless-perfect?

One day I read Bishop H. C. G. Moule's commentary on Philippians. I cannot quote him because he used such big words; it is beyond me. I can only tell you that in the third chapter of

Philippians he raised this question. He said that some people believe in idealistic perfectionism. They believe that they can be sinless-perfect. So far as our spiritual position is concerned we are in Christ and in Him we are complete; we are perfect. That gives us glory, and that is our boast in Christ Jesus. But when you come to your spiritual condition—not position but condition—even with all the fulness of grace, you cannot but see your own imperfection. You have such a vision of the glory of the Lord, of the absolute holiness of God, and that vision keeps you from falling. It gives you hope but also it tells you that you are still imperfect. On the one hand, we rejoice in the Lord; on the other hand, we humble ourselves before Him, pressing on towards the goal. That was the gist of what he said.

WALK IN THE LIGHT

"If we walk in the light as He is in the light, we have fellowship with one another, and the blood of Jesus Christ God's Son cleanses us from all sin" (I John 1:7). "If we walk in the light." The light there is not the Word of God. True, the

Word of God is light; it is a lamp shining before our feet, and by the guidance of that light we may walk uprightly. But in I John it says, "God is light." Not only is His Word light, God Himself is light, and that points to the life of God. The life of God is light. Because we have the life of God, we have the life of Christ in us, if we walk in the light as God dwells in the light, this life of Christ will shine within us. Now there is a difference here.

Sometimes we try to illustrate it. God is like a hundred candlelights—full, absolute, unlimited, without measure. That is God. His life is so bright. There is no darkness, no shadow, no turning, and no one can see God who dwells in that unapproachable light. But "if we walk in the light"—the light here is one candlelight. We are just saved; we just received the life of Christ in us. Even though that life is a matured life, yet so far as our experience of that life is concerned, it is just the beginning. So we say that we only have one candlelight. That is all we know about Him and His life. But if we walk in that one candlelight, as God dwells in the hundred candlelights, we can have fellowship one with another. There is such a difference in degree, in measure, but there is the same quality. And because the quality is the same, God condescends to our level and fellowships with us. The wonderful thing is that if we walk in the light we already have, invariably that light will show us how imperfect we are. That light will show us where our sin is, where our shortcoming is, where our failure is, and when light exposes our darkness, thank God the blood of God's Son, Jesus Christ, cleanses us from all our sins. So we can fellowship with God.

But we cannot remain in that one candlelight; we have to grow. As we grow in the knowledge of our Lord Jesus and begin to know His perfect life in us more, it becomes two candlelights. What happens? In those two candlelights you discover more shortcomings, more failures. Some hidden parts, unknown parts begin to be revealed. God does not reveal everything to us at the same time. If He did, we would die. But gradually, He will purify us. Gradually, He will shed His light upon us so that we may repent, return, and the blood of the Lord Jesus will cleanse us from all our sins. And by that we have fellowship. Then we grow again. This is Christian life.

We can never come to a place as long as we are in this flesh, in this body, where we say that we are now sinless-perfect. If we do, we deceive ourselves. Thank God, when our Lord Jesus went to the cross, He bore all the sins that we have committed upon His own body, and there He was crucified, He died, and shed His blood for the remission of our sins.

But what about the sinful nature that we inherited from our forefather, Adam? All the outward acts of sins have been forgiven, as if we had never sinned. But unfortunately, the sinful nature is still in us. As long as we are in this body, the sinful nature is there. We will not be delivered until we are delivered from this mortal body. But thank God, there is a way. It is not by eradication, because if it were we would become careless and say, "Now I am perfect. I am sinless-perfect." We would be proud of ourselves. We would deceive ourselves, and that would be the end of our spiritual life. But thank God, God allows this sinful nature to remain in us in order to prove us, that we may be humbled, that we may look up to Him, knowing that without Him we can do nothing. This leads us into holiness, into sanctification.

PERFECT MEANS MATURED

I think first of all, we need to settle this question. When the Scripture speaks of perfection in relation to man it does not mean sinless perfection. What does it mean then? I went to *Vine's Word Dictionary of the New Testament*, and there he gives the meaning of the word *perfect*. He said that the word *perfect* in Greek means, "having reached the end." Therefore it means "finished, complete, perfect." When this word is applied to man, it means either of two things. One, it means "matured, grown-up, full-grown, into manhood."

You will find this in a number of Scriptures. For instance, in I Corinthians 2:2 the apostle Paul said to the Corinthians, "I know nothing among you save Jesus Christ and Him crucified." He taught nothing among them but Jesus Christ and Him crucified.

17

In verse 6 he said, "But we speak wisdom among the perfect." The Corinthian believers were babes in Christ, so he had to speak to them exclusively of the foundational truth. But he said, "Among the perfect, among the grown-up we do speak of wisdom, not of this world but of wisdom of the mystery of God."

Again, you will find in I Corinthians 14:20, he said, "Brethren, be not children [babes] in your minds, but in malice be babes; but in your minds be grown-up, [be perfect]."

In Ephesians 4:13 it says, "That we may all arrive at the unity of the faith and of the knowledge of the Son of God, that we may be full grown, to the measure of the stature of the fulness of Christ." So there you have the word *full grown, perfect.*

In Colossians 1:28 Paul desires to present the saints perfect in Christ Jesus, full grown in Christ Jesus. That is one meaning of *perfect*—"grown up, matured, full grown."

PERFECT MEANS GOODNESS

Perfect has another meaning. It means "goodness"; not necessarily matured but goodness. In other words, it tells of some character of God, some character of Christ being shown in the life of man.

Matthew 5:48 is in that category: "Be ye perfect as the heavenly Father is perfect." In that section of Matthew 5, what is He talking about? He is talking about the love of God. He says that God loves everyone. If we only love the ones that are dear to us and hate our enemies, it is not like God because God loves everyone. He gives rain to the evil as well as to the good. So, "Be ye perfect as your heavenly Father is perfect." In other words, it is all about love and that we may bear some measure of the same character of love that is of God.

In Matthew 19, a young man came to the Lord and said, "Lord, what shall I do that I may inherit eternal life?" And the Lord talked to him about the commandments: Honor your father and mother, and so on. And the young man said, "I have kept all these from my youth." The Lord looked at him with love and said, "If you want to be perfect, sell all that you have, give to the poor, and then come and follow me." The Lord knew that his wealth hindered him from following the Lord, and following the Lord all the way is the way to perfection. So here it also refers to goodness or character.

In the book of James it says, "If anyone can control his tongue he is a perfect man." It speaks of character.

We find that what the Bible teaches about perfection in man is not sinless perfection but it is growing up in the life of Christ that is in you, so that your life bears the character of the Lord Jesus. That is the teaching of the Word of God.

PERFECTION IS GOD'S WILL

Why is it that we need to be perfect? Sometimes we naturally have a kind of mentality: if only we can be saved, then we will not go to hell but go to heaven. Just like one person said, "If my two legs get within the door of heaven I will be satisfied." That is our mentality, but this is the mentality of a baby. God wants us to be grown up. Why is it that we need to be perfect? After we are saved, why not just sit back and enjoy ourselves? After all, we will go to heaven. But this is not the will of God. What is the will of God concerning His people? Is God satisfied with us just getting saved and remaining as babes in Christ? To be a babe, of course, is very comfortable. There is no responsibility and everyone has to take care of you, but you fail in the purpose of God for your life. What is God's will?

In Romans 8:29 we are told: "Whom he has foreknown, he has predestinated to be conformed to the image of his beloved Son, that His Son may be the firstborn among many brethren." In other words, God has predestined us not just to be justified, saved, and that's it. God has predestined us, chosen us, elected us that we may be conformed to the image of His beloved Son. It is that we may have His likeness, we may be like Him, and He may be the firstborn among many brethren because many are like Him, taking up His character; not only His likeness but the character of that life. That is the will of God.

So if among us there are some who still have that babyish mentality, remember how you hurt the heart of God. We must pursue after perfection. We must grow from babies to young people, from young people to the elders because this is the will of God.

PERFECTION IS GOD'S COMMAND

Furthermore, not only is "to be perfect" God's will, remember it is God's command. "Be ye perfect, therefore as your heavenly Father is perfect." It is a command. If you love the Lord, the Lord said, "Keep My commandments." Oftentimes we hear brothers and sisters in their prayers say, "Lord, how I love You." Thank God, for that expression, but sometimes it would be good for us to sit down and meditate. Do I really love Him as I said? How do I know if I love Him? If I disobey Him, if I go my own way, if I do not keep His Word, His commandments, do I love Him? "If you love Me keep My commandments."

I cannot help but remember the story of C. T. Studd who was one of the seven Cambridge graduates who went out to China together as missionaries. It stirred the student world at that time. C. T. Studd visited Edinburgh where F. B. Meyer, another brilliant young man, was pastor. It was in November in Edinburgh, Scotland, and it was very chilly, very cold. C. T. Studd got up at 4:00 in the morning, which was his habit. He lit the candle and read the Word of God and had communion with God. F. B. Meyer, being the host, saw the light in C. T. Studd's room and was worried whether his guest had some problem. But it was so early that he did not dare knock on the door. He waited and waited until he could not wait any more. He knocked on the door and when he went in, he saw C. T. Studd wrapped up in a rug because it was cold. F. B. Meyer said, "You got up early."

"Oh," he said, "I love the Lord; I am searching the Scriptures for His commandments that I may keep them." That touched F. B. Meyer very deeply.

Does it touch you? We search the Scriptures for promises. Sometimes we are even too lazy to search and we get a promise box and just pick one up. But this man loved the Lord and he proved his love by searching the Scriptures for

23

God's commandments that he may keep them. Remember, "to be perfect" is God's command. We should not neglect it. If you love Him, keep His commandment.

PERFECTION IS THE WORK OF THE SPIRIT

And thank God, to be perfect is the very work of the indwelling Holy Spirit. We have the Holy Spirit dwelling in us. He is the Spirit of Christ. What is His work in us? He is in us, not as a guest; He is in us as our Teacher, as our resident Boss. What is He doing in us? What is His work day and night without ceasing, in the small things and great things? He is teaching us of Christ. He is transforming us from glory to glory, that we may be like Christ. That is the work of the Holy Spirit.

To be perfect is something beyond us. In other words, no one is able to improve himself to be perfect. No matter how strong your will power is, you will fail. But thank God, it is the work of the Holy Spirit, and He is in each one of us doing this one work: glorifying Christ. What do you mean by glorifying Christ? Glorifying Christ simply means that Christ may be formed in you. That is glorifying Christ and that is the work of the Holy Spirit. We need to trust Him. How often we will not listen to His voice! How often we grieve Him! But that is the very work He is doing in us.

In Colossians you find that this is the very work of the apostle Paul. In other words, what is spiritual ministry? Spiritual ministry is with all means to bring people to be perfect in Christ Jesus. So any ministry that is less than this does not fulfill spiritual ministry.

Now, with all this are you convinced that it is God's will for you to be perfect? Can you say it is all right for you not to be perfect? Is there any excuse? I hope not.

Finally, we would like to ask a question. How do we know that we are on the way to perfection? Are there any signs telling us that we are on the right course? I think we want to know that.

SIGNS OF PERFECTION

Number one: in I Corinthians 13:8-12 it says, "Love never fails; but whether prophecies, they shall be done away; or tongues, they shall cease; or knowledge, it shall be done away. For we know in part, and we prophesy in part: but when that which is perfect has come, that which is in part shall be done away. When I was a child, I spoke as a child, I felt as a child, I reasoned as a child; when I became a man, I had done with what belonged to the child."

I want to borrow these verses to see the principle behind it. The principle behind these verses is that the sign of being perfect is love. We often think to be grown up is knowledge—if I know. Or maybe we even think it is prophecy— if I am able to utter it, to explain it, that shows I am matured. But that is wrong. Knowledge puffs up; love builds up. He who thinks he knows, he does not know. But he who loves is known of God. So the sign of growing up is love. How much of the love of Christ is in your life and demonstrated? How much do you really love the Lord with all your heart, with all your understanding, with all your strength? How much do you love your brothers? How much of the love of God do you know and experience and express? That is the first sign of growing up.

Number two: in Philippians 3:15 it says, "As many therefore as are perfect, let us be thus minded; and if ye are any otherwise minded, this also God shall reveal to you." In other words, the second sign of growing up in the Lord is a renewed mind, a mind that is like the mind of Christ, a mind that has been demonstrated in the life of Paul. He considered everything as dross for the excellency of that living, experiential knowledge of our Lord Jesus.

Number 3: I Corinthians 2:6a, 7a: "But we speak wisdom among the perfect; but wisdom not of this world...God's wisdom in a mystery." And when you read on you find it is concerned with the eternal purpose of God. People who show that they really enter into that wisdom, it is a sign of maturity. So may the Lord help us.

Shall we pray:

Dear Lord, our prayer is that Thou will make it unmistakably clear to each one of us, what Thou dost demand of us. Oh Lord, when Thou said, "Be thou perfect," show us what it really means. And Lord, we desire it. We will cooperate with Thy

Holy Spirit who alone can do this work. Bless Thy people, we ask in Thy precious name. Amen.

THE WAY TO
SPIRITUAL PERFECTION

Philippians 3:15—As many therefore as are perfect, let us be thus minded; and if ye are any otherwise minded, this also God shall reveal to you.

Shall we pray:

Dear Lord, our hearts are full of thanks. We are so thankful for all that Thou has done for us. Thou has not kept anything from us. Thou givest Thy blood, Thy flesh, to us, Thyself wholly to us. Lord, who are we that Thou should be mindful of us? How we praise and thank Thee for what Thou has done on Calvary's cross. We thank Thee that it is finished. There is nothing that can be added or be taken away. Grant us that vision. Give us that understanding. Enable us to have full faith and confidence in Thee, and draw us that we may truly run after Thee. Dear Lord, we do want to glorify Thee, and we want to see Thy image being formed in us that Thou may be glorified. Hear our cry. We commit ourselves to Thee again for this time, trusting Thy Holy Spirit to reveal Thy heart and Thy mind to us. Lead us into Thy truth, and we will give Thee all the glory. We ask in the name of our dear Lord Jesus Christ. Amen.

I find it very difficult to speak after the Lord's Table because the Lord's Table is really the climax. We have been brought to His very presence. We see anew, afresh what He has done for us, and it is a perfect work. Nothing can be added. If only we have faith and trust Him for what He has done for us, I do not think there is any need to talk any more. So that is why I always find it very, very difficult to speak after the Lord's Table. If our hearts are really filled with Him, what else do we need? What else are we seeking for? But because I have not finished my burden, I have to continue.

Our theme for this time is: Spiritual Perfection, but it is actually more than just a theme to talk about; it is something that is vital to our Christian life. We are limited by ourselves, by our thinking, by our concepts, by our needs. So we always feel that if only God would do something to satisfy our need or to solve our problem, we will be satisfied. We do not want anything more than that. But we must remember that God created us and He redeemed us with a very specific purpose. It is for His glory, and He will not be satisfied until His glory is manifested in us. He will continue to work in our lives until Christ is fully formed in us. That is glory; that is His character that fits with Himself. God does not want us to stop midway. He wants us to arrive at the end, and the end is God's purpose in love for His people.

We believe spiritual perfection is God's will for all His people, not just for a few, selected, special, so-called spiritual giants. It is for every child of God. God expects every child of God to grow up into maturity, and if any one of us would be complacent and satisfied with anything short of that I think it would grieve the heart of God. So I do hope that at least for this moment we do have a desire for spiritual perfection. It is not sinless perfection but it is something that would answer the heart of God. God is perfect and He expects us to be perfect; not in the same degree or measure, but in the same quality and nature.

OBTAINMENT

Now I would like to go into this matter of the way to spiritual perfection. First of all I would like to pose a question. I hope you will listen very carefully. Is spiritual perfection something to be obtained or something to be attained? What is meant by obtained? *Obtained* means that everything is already ready. It is a gift, freely given, universally given. You do not need to do anything. There is nothing required of you. All you need to do is receive it by faith. That is obtainment.

It is just like our salvation. We do not need to do anything. As a matter of fact, the more you try to do, the farther away you are from the salvation of the Lord because it is a gift. Everything is prepared for you. On Calvary's cross our Lord Jesus has borne your sins in His own body. Just believe in Him and your sins are all forgiven. You are justified before God. If you believe on the Lord Jesus you have life. You receive eternal life—the life of God, the life of

Christ. His very life will come into you and you are born again. You do not need to do anything and you cannot do anything. It is a free gift. So it is something to be obtained. Everything is ready; there is nothing more to be done. Just receive it by faith and it is yours.

ATTAINMENT

What is attainment? *Attainment* means there is a goal before you and you have to run after it. You have to strive to arrive at the goal. A promise is there but you have to attain to that promise.

So, is spiritual perfection obtained or attained? Probably after you have listened for the past day you are a little confused. On the one hand, you have heard that everything is done. Our brother mentioned the new covenant. It is done. It is the work of God, accomplished in His Son, Jesus Christ. It is finished. You cannot add anything to the new covenant. It is all there—absolute, unconditional, inward, intimate. It is ready to be given to you. And from God's standpoint, He has already given it. All you need to do is accept it, receive it, and it is yours. You have spiritual perfection.

Then, probably you heard how we need to strive, how we need to put ourselves in it, how we need to be diligent before we can really achieve that spiritual perfection. Is there any contradiction? So far as I am concerned, I believe that spiritual perfection is both to be obtained and to be attained. It is both.

OBJECTIVE TRUTH

Objective truth is something that God has done in His beloved Son and it is finished. The work of our Lord Jesus on Calvary's cross is eternal truth. Whatever He has done on the cross remains forever. Time will not change it, circumstance will not change it, and condition will not change it. Nothing can change it; it is there standing forever—no shadow, no shade. It is truth forever. It is absolute. That is spiritual truth, and our foundation is laid on spiritual truth. Without that foundation, there is nothing to build upon. Without that foundation, whatever we have done will be false. It does not depend upon your condition. Whether you believe it or not does not matter. Just because you do not believe in it, does not mean it has lost its power. It is still as powerful as it was on that day when our Lord Jesus was crucified. This is objective truth. This is something of which we need to have a very clear view. There should be no doubt in our hearts. And this is our foundation.

SUBJECTIVE EXPERIENCE

On the other hand, we find the experiential side. So far as our experience is concerned, that is subjective. Objective is something already done; it is forever there; it is eternal truth; it never changes. But subjective experience is personal. In other words, it is a condition of our spiritual life and it changes. It should be progressive, and it is something that you have to use diligence in order to arrive at the goal. So these are the two sides in the Word of God.

On the one hand, we have to lay hold of the objective truth given in the Scriptures; the firmer the hold the better. On the other hand, if we lay hold on that firm foundation there is bound to be personal experience. Or to put it in another way, objective truth is God's work in His Son; subjective experience is God's work through His Holy Spirit. Objective truth is what God has done in His Son on Calvary's cross; subjective experience is what the Holy Spirit is working in each of our lives today. And if it is real spiritual experience, it is to experience what the objective truth tells us. In other words, it is not just something far away. The Holy Spirit brings what Christ has done two thousand years ago into our very daily experience, and this takes time. It requires cooperation.

REVELATION

In this matter of spiritual maturity I believe we need a revelation of our Lord Jesus. We need to have a revelation of the completeness of His work, the new covenant established by His very blood. We need to know our Lord Jesus as the mediator of the new covenant, and the clearer we are the better. We need to have full faith in what the Lord has done for us on Calvary's cross. And if that were all, how good it would be! We would have no responsibility. We would not need to go through the process, sometimes very painful, and we would already be there. Sometimes I have thought that after I was saved if I were immediately raptured to heaven, how good that would be! Why does the Lord leave me here on earth, and leave me so long? Well, He has a purpose. He is bringing what Christ has done on Calvary's cross into my very being.

You know, I was brought up in a Christian family, and I read the Bible before I was saved. My father would lead the daily devotions. He would read from a big Bible, and then we would all kneel down and he would lead us in prayer. So from my childhood I knew the Bible, but even so, the Bible was like Greek to me. I did not understand it. I read it. I knew it. I believed it. I never doubted the Bible as the Word of God. But somehow it did not work. The Bible is the Bible and I am myself—two separate entities. But thank God, that afternoon I was saved, I went into my room, opened my Bible and it was II Peter 1. Somehow it spoke to my heart. It was different. It was the living Word because a relationship was there.

THE GIFT OF GOD

In II Peter 1:3 it says, "As his divine power has given to us all things which relate to life and godliness, through the knowledge of him that has called us by glory and virtue, through which he has given to us the greatest and precious promises, that through these ye may become partakers of the divine nature, having escaped the corruption that is in the world through lust."

When you read these verses, what is the impression that they give you? Here it says very clearly, "As his divine power has given." In other words, it starts with God. His divine power has given to us all things. Everything which relates to life and godliness is given by Him. The life here of course is eternal life—the life of Christ, God's own life, spiritual life. All things regarding life have been given. Life has been given. Everything that life is, is there.

"And godliness." What is godliness? Godliness simply means "like God." How can we be like God if there is no life? But with that life, God has given to us everything concerning godliness. How can we be like God? All the

38

power is there. All the elements are there. All the potential is there. It is freely given, and this is given through the knowledge of Him who has called us. And the knowledge here is not book knowledge or mental knowledge. The knowledge here is experiential knowledge, intimate knowledge, personal knowledge. We know God has given us all things regarding life and godliness—life given as a beginning, godliness given as the end.

All have been given "through the knowledge of the one who has called us by glory and virtue" (v. 3b). We are all called by God. And when God calls us, He calls us by His glory. In other words, His calling is according to what He is. He is glory; therefore when He called us, He called us to glory. Anything short of glory is short of His calling.

"And virtue" (II Peter 1:4a). The virtue here is especially related to His work. In other words, He called us according to His glory and He works to bring us into that glory.

"Through which He has given to us" (v. 4b). Again, when God gives, it is a free gift. There is no condition, no requirement. He does it all.

"He has given to us the greatest and precious promises" (v. 4c). All through the Word of God, you find not only great but greatest promises, not only promises but precious promises concerning this matter of life and godliness. Our Lord said, "Come to Me. He that believes in Me has eternal life." What a promise that is! And thank God, not only has He given us greatest and precious promises concerning life and godliness, which is spiritual perfection, He has put all these promises into a covenant, into a contract, into something that is binding to Himself. In other words, He condescends Himself to our level. He knows what little faith we have, how suspicious we are. We cannot believe anybody. So He binds Himself and puts His promises into a contract, into an everlasting covenant to assure us that it shall be done. And "through these ye may become partakers of the divine nature" (v. 4d). That is spiritual perfection.

So from these two verses we see that spiritual perfection is the gift of God. It is not only promised, it is accomplished in His Son and given to us. Spiritual perfection is to be obtained. Everything is ready; just receive it. Thank God for it! That is our blessed hope. That gives us joy, strength.

HUMAN RESPONSIBILITY

"But for this very reason also" (v. 5a). It is not about something else; it is from this very thing—life and godliness, partakers of His divine nature, delivered from the world and lust. In this very matter, for this very reason—for the very reason that God has given these promises—He has given us all things concerning life and godliness. For this very reason also, "using therewith all diligence" (v. 5b).

In verses 3-4, it is all that God has done. We do nothing; it is a gift, and we receive. But from verse 5-11 it seems as if it begins to shift to us. We need to use all diligence. We need to supply that diligence. God has given but if we do not supply diligence we will not get it. So this is human responsibility. God requires us to cooperate with Him. In the final analysis it is still His grace, but His grace works in us to enable us to co-operate with Him. So here you find we need to use all diligence.

If spiritual perfection is given by God to all, why is it that not all exhibit, manifest, express spiritual perfection? Why is it that today among God's people there are more babies than grown-ups? Why is it? It is because most people do not use diligence. They just sit back and try to have an easy time instead of applying themselves to what God has promised, for what Christ has accomplished, applying ourselves, desiring it, pursuing it, seeking for it diligently.

"In your faith have also virtue" (v. 5c). If you have faith, if you believe, then faith without work is dead. If it is living faith, there is the work of faith following. It is there.

"In virtue knowledge" (v. 6a). You need to know the mind of God. If you want to work, you have to work according to His will, so you need knowledge.

"In knowledge temperance" (v. 6b)— self-control.

"In temperance endurance" (v. 6c). There is suffering involved.

"In endurance godliness, in godliness brotherly love, in brotherly love love" (v. 6d-7).

So you find this life in us has all these qualities—the life of Christ in us has faith, virtue, knowledge, temperance, endurance, godliness, brotherly love, and love. All these qualities are in that life, but that life needs to be developed. It needs to grow so that all these things will begin to appear and be manifested.

"For these things existing and abounding in you make you to be neither idle nor unfruitful as regards the knowledge of our Lord Jesus Christ" (v. 8).

If we say we know the Lord Jesus, then invariably all these qualities will appear, but we need to be diligent about it.

"For he with whom these things are not present is blind" (v. 9a). Spiritual seeing is most practical. What is unseen can be seen. What is invisible is made visible. The life of Christ in us is unseen but it has to be visible. That is testimony. Otherwise we are blind. We think we have it but we do not. We are shortsighted, living just for this world.

"And has forgotten the purging of his former sins" (v. 9b). We even forget how the Lord has forgiven us our sins.

"Wherefore the rather, brethren, use diligence to make your calling and election sure" (v. 10). Thank God we have a calling. It is a calling to glory, to spiritual perfection. We are elected by God for that purpose, but we have to make our calling and election sure.

"For doing these things ye will never fall; for thus shall the entrance into the everlasting kingdom of our Lord and Saviour Jesus Christ be richly furnished unto you" (v. 10b-11).

So you see that in the very Word of God there are these two sides and they complement each other. They do not contradict each other. We need to put our full confidence in what our Lord has done for us. And if we have that confidence, then we will apply ourselves to yield to the Holy Spirit in our daily life.

So I hope we will not have a kind of confusion among us. Thank God it is both. One is absolute; that is the truth. One is relative; that is our experience. When you think of what God has done in Christ for us, it gives us hope, it gives us joy. But it should draw us, giving us that desire to seek diligently for it.

THE EXPERIENTIAL SIDE

I would like to just mention a few things from the experiential side. When you do that you have to take for granted that the truth side is already established. If the truth side is not established there is nothing to build on. The Holy Spirit can only work upon what Christ has accomplished. So I do hope we have a firm foundation of what Christ has done for us, and on that basis we will pursue it. I will mention just a few things on the subjective side, how in our daily life we can arrive at the spiritual perfection that God is calling us into.

MADE PERFECT IN CHRIST

Of course, spiritual perfection is a Person. Spiritual perfection is Christ. Christ has already demonstrated to us while He was on earth. He is the only one who is spiritually perfect, absolutely perfect. So when we talk about spiritual perfection, it means that it is only in Him that we are made perfect. If it is not in Him, nothing can be perfect. So we need to know Him. If we know Him, He will bring us into spiritual perfection because He is that perfection.

CONSECRATION

In Philippians 3 you find that what the apostle Paul considered as precious and important in his life in the past, completely changed when the Lord met him on the road to Damascus. The glory of the Lord took hold of that young man and he completely surrendered himself to the Lord. In that surrender something happened; his mind was renewed. In other words, before that his mind was set upon the world and the things of the world. These were life to him. But after the Lord met him on the road to Damascus, in his surrender his mind

46

underwent a change. Now he said, "I look at all things as dross, as refuse for the excellency of the knowledge of Jesus Christ." To know Him became His passion.

In the way to spiritual perfection our mind plays a very essential part. If our mind is not renewed, we will not be able to walk in this way of spiritual perfection. We will go where our mind is set. But we cannot change our mind. Only the Holy Spirit can do that on one condition—consecration, surrender. Consecration is very, very basic to our Christian life. If we really want to grow in the Lord, in the knowledge of the Lord, which will bring growth in our lives, we need to present our bodies a living sacrifice. We need to give ourselves completely to the Lord. We need to hand over ourselves, our right to ourselves: "Lord, this is Yours. You have bought it with a price. Do whatever You like according to Your will."

When we think of consecration, sometimes we are afraid, thinking that by consecrating ourselves we lose everything. But thank God, what we lose is something that needs to be lost; what we gain cannot be measured.

So in my heart I feel that unless we really consecrate ourselves to the Lord there is no way to spiritual perfection. Our mind has to be renewed, and when we consecrate ourselves, the Holy Spirit renews our mind. That is Romans 12:1-2.

Young people, you are told by your elders: "Do not love the world. Do not be conformed to the world." But can you do it? You just love it. You may outwardly obey, but when you become independent, you will be worse than the worldly people, seeking after the world. We tell the young people: "Do the will of God." Once I asked a young person, "What do you think about the will of God?" He said, "Everything that is against me is the will of God." Can you love the will of God? Can you prove it? Of course not! But with the renewing of the mind, it is different. You look at the world as dross and you look at the knowledge of the Lord Jesus as the most precious thing in your life. So it is absolute surrender. Do not hold back anything from the

Lord. So far as you know give yourself completely to the Lord. Let the Lord have every key to your life, and if you are not willing pray as F. B. Meyer prayed: "Lord, make me willing to be willing."

ABIDING

Secondly, if you want to know somebody, you have to live very close to that person. So in the Scripture the Lord said, "Abide in Me and I in you." That is the secret. Spiritual experience is very simple. Just learn to abide in Christ. It is not those crises, special experiences that count. It is your daily abiding that counts. When the first two disciples, John and Andrew, followed the Lord, the Lord turned back and said, "What do you want?" They said, "Where do You live? We want to abide with You." And that abiding made John what he was. He knew the Lord much more intimately than the others.

How do we abide in Him? daily abide in Him? Once I asked young people: "How do you abide in the Lord?" Some said, "Well, we need to read the Bible every day. We need to pray. We need to go to meetings, have fellowship." All these are true, but the secret of abiding is in I John 2:27. It says, "The anointing is in you." Obey the anointing, and you will abide in Christ. Thank God the Holy Spirit is in us. He is there to bring us into glory, to transform us. He is there to make Christ known to us. Whatever is not of Christ He will show us. Whatever is of Christ He will also reveal to us. All you need to do in your daily life—big things, small things—is obey the voice of the Holy Spirit within you. That is the way to spiritual perfection.

DISCIPLINE

Another thing is the matter of discipline. You do not like to hear this word, but discipline is necessary for growth (see Hebrews 12). Discipline involves suffering because there is so much in us that is old, natural, earthly, worldly, selfish, even satanic. And all these things in us have to go. But when they go, we suffer in our flesh. But it is necessary because the Holy Spirit is not only negatively taking away all these things that stand in the way of spiritual perfection, at the same time He is adding Christ into us. Discipline is important. Do not despise discipline. It is the love of the Father so that we can be partakers of His divine nature.

THE BODY OF CHRIST

Finally, this matter of spiritual maturity is more than a personal experience. Why is it that we are not as absolutely perfect as Christ is perfect? We can have a measure of His perfection. It is because we are limited. Man is limited in his capacity, so we can only contain so much of the riches of Christ in us. These riches of Christ, the fulness of Christ, the perfection of Christ can only be expressed through a body. So you find in Ephesians 4:13: "Until we all arrive at the unity of the faith and of the knowledge of the Son of God, at the full-grown man, at the measure of the stature of the fulness of the Christ."

This can only be reached in the body of Christ. Therefore we cannot afford to be independent, thinking that we alone are sufficient. We need our brothers and sisters. We need fellowship. We need to be helped by our brothers and sisters. What you do not have, they have. They can share with you. And what God has graciously given to you, you can share with your brothers and sisters. That is the way we grow together into the fulness of the stature of our Lord Jesus. So may the Lord help us.

Shall we pray:

Dear Lord, we want to thank Thee because Thy Word is perfect. We thank Thee for what Thou has done for us—so complete. We thank Thee for what the Holy Spirit is doing in us so patiently, so persistently, until what Christ has done on the cross is fully realized in Thy body. Oh Lord, may Thy bride be made ready to meet the Bridegroom. We ask in Thy precious name. Amen.

QUESTION AND ANSWER

Q: Does the church have to be perfected before Christ can return?

This question is very simple, but when you think about it, it is very hard, very complicated. We do believe that the return of our Lord Jesus is very closely related to the completion of the church because the Bridegroom cannot be married to a bride that is not mature. So our Lord Jesus, as the Bridegroom, looks for a bride who will be His counterpart, His like. The Bible tells us how He will sanctify the church, purify the church by the water of the word that the church may be glorious, without spot or wrinkle or any of such sort, holy and blameless, to be presented to Him as His bride. So I think the question in one sense is very simple. The church must be completed, must be perfect in order that she may be married to the Bridegroom who is Himself perfect.

This is a good question, and it has been asked by many people. If we wait until the church is complete, is perfect, how long will we have to wait? Our Lord Jesus has waited for her two thousand years already, and the more we look at the condition of the church in general, the more discouraged we are. Brother Sparks once asked brother Nee a question: "What is the most difficult prophecy to be fulfilled in the Bible? And brother Nee's answer was Ephesians 5. And that is very true. But God cannot fail.

The Lord said, "I will build My church." And when He builds, He will never do anything incomplete, unfinished. So we believe that before the coming of the Lord, the church must be brought to spiritual perfection, must be brought to maturity, full grown, to be like Him. When you look at outward situations, you may be discouraged, but with your eyes of faith, seeing that our Lord is working, you are encouraged because the Lord has His hidden ones everywhere upon this earth. And if we have the eyes of faith we can see that He is completing the church.

As you read the book of Revelation, you find there are two places where the bride has made herself ready for the Bridegroom. One is in Revelation 19 and the other is in Revelation 21. Now you wonder whether this is one incident or if these are two difference incidences. There may be different interpretations. So far as I understand, chapter 19 happens at the beginning of the millenium, the coming age when the kingdom of God comes upon this earth. In that time period the Bible says, "The bride has made herself ready, and she was given bright, shining, white linen garments which are the righteousnesses of the saints." So here you find the bride is ready before the wedding, and she has made herself ready. That is her responsibility. But immediately He said, "She was given." It was the grace of God that enabled her to be ready, to respond, and she was to be clothed with a wedding garment which is the righteousnesses of the saints.

We know that Christ is our righteousness. We are clothed with Christ. That is our standing before God, but over and above that, the church has to have a wedding garment. It is an embroidered garment, the work of the Holy Spirit. How He patiently works until that garment is finished. It is called the righteousnesses of the saints. We have no righteousness of our own. Christ is our righteousness. But the Holy Spirit takes the life of Christ in us and works patiently in us until there comes righteousnesses as the righteousness of our Lord Jesus. This is the wedding garment. In other words, the bride is conformed to the image of the Bridegroom. But that will happen before the millenium. It introduces the millenium, the coming age.

Who is that bride that has made herself ready? Is every believer at that moment ready to be the bride? Is every believer at that time clothed with the wedding garment? That is a very serious question. Unfortunately, as a matter of fact, we find this is not so. Probably, at that time it is only a remnant, the overcomers of the church, because you remember in Revelation 2-3 there is the call to overcome. So far as the general condition of the church is concerned, it has not been completed, but thank God, there are those in the church who overcome because of the blood of the Lamb, the word of their testimony, and they love not their lives even unto death. Personally, I believe they are the first fruits of the church and they are ready. And when they are ready, the Bridegroom will come.

In Revelation 12, when the manchild is born, he is caught up to the throne, and when he is caught up to the throne, there will be war in the air. Satan will be thrown upon this earth. In other words, God is preparing the air for the coming of the Lord. He will come from the throne to the air, invisible, and from the air to the Mount of Olives, visible.

God's Word stands forever. What He said will be done. And personally I believe at the end of this age the overcomers, the first fruits of the church will be ready, and when they are ready, Christ shall return.

But thank God, because again we find in Revelation 21 the bride of the Lamb, the New Jerusalem descending upon the new heaven and new earth. Of course, we know this is eternity. After the millenium, which is the coming age, comes eternity. And who is the bride in eternity?

The bride is prepared for the Bridegroom, and by that word *prepared* you know she is ready, completed, perfect. She is the New Jerusalem, bearing the glory of God with the twelve foundations, the twelve names of the apostles, and the twelve gates with the names of the twelve tribes of Israel. In other words, in eternity all the work of God throughout the centuries will be gathered together, summed up, consummated into that bride of the Lamb, and this is eternity.

Romans 8:29 must be fulfilled: "Whom God has foreknown, He has foreordained that they may be conformed to the image of His beloved Son, that His Son may be the first born among many brethren." When He begins to work in us, He will not stop until it is fully completed. So thank God for that. But hopefully, today we may learn to cooperate with the grace that God has given to us, respond to His grace, and be prepared and ready to receive the Bridegroom.

Other Books Printed By
Christian Testimony Ministry

Speaker	Title
Dana Congdon	Marriage, Singleness, and the Will of God
	Recovery & Restoration
	The Holy Spirit
	Hebrews
A.J. Flack	Tent of His Splendour
Stephen Kaung	Acts
	Be Ye Therefore Perfect
	Called Out Unto Christ
	Called to the Fellowship of God's Son
	Divine Life and Order
	For Me to Live is Christ
	Glorious Liberty of the Children of God
	God's Purpose for the Family
	I Will Build My Church
	Meditations on the Kingdom
	Recovery
	Spiritual Exercise
	Spiritual Life (II Corinthians Series)
	Teach Us to Pray
	The Cross
	The Fulness of Christ—In the Book of Revelation
	The Headship of Christ
	The Kingdom and the Church
	The Kingdom of God
	The Last Call to the Churches, the Call to Overcome
	The Life of Our Lord Jesus
	The Life of the Church, the Body of Christ
	The Lord's Table
	Two Guideposts for Inheriting the Kingdom
	Vision of Christ (Revelation)
	Who Are We?

WHY DO WE SO GATHER?
WORSHIP

LANCE LAMBERT

CALLED UNTO HIS ETERNAL GLORY
GOD'S ETERNAL PURPOSE
IN THE DAY OF THY POWER
JACOB I HAVE LOVED
LIVING FAITH
LESSONS FROM THE LIFE OF MOSES
LOVE DIVINE
MY HOUSE SHALL BE A HOUSE OF PRAYER
PREPARATION FOR THE COMING OF THE LORD
REIGNING WITH CHRIST
SPIRITUAL CHARACTER
THE GOSPEL OF THE KINGDOM
THE IMPORTANCE OF COVERING
THE LAST DAYS AND GOD'S PRIORITIES
THE PRIZE
THE SUPREMACY OF JESUS CHRIST
THINE IS THE POWER!
THOU ART MINE

T. AUSTIN-SPARKS

THE LORD'S TESTIMONY AND THE WORLD NEED

HARVEY CEDARS CONFERENCE

STEPHEN KAUNG

HEAVENLY VISION
SPIRITUAL RESPONSIBILITY

CONGDON, HILE, KAUNG

SPIRITUAL MINISTRY
SPIRITUAL AUTHORITY
SPIRITUAL HOUSE
SPIRITUAL SUBMISSION

STEPHEN KAUNG

SPIRITUAL KNOWLEDGE
SPIRITUAL POWER
SPIRITUAL REALITY
SPIRITUAL VALUE
SPIRITUAL BLESSING
SPIRITUAL DISCERNMENT

9 781942 521556